A DAY IN THE LIFE AS A GOVERNMENT WORKER

By Anonymous Author

The following stories are actual events and experiences shared by employees of the Federal, State, or other local government. The incidents include everything from acquiring employment with the government, to events which arise while employed by the government. Names of the participants have been withheld for their protection against retaliation by their employer. Each participant has been assigned a number rather than being called by name.

Names of employees involved in any of the following incidents have also been changed for their protection. Specific times, dates or places will be altered or removed to avoid participants being targeted by their employer for retaliation. This writing is strictly informatory, and is in no way intended to discredit the government. Participants wish only to share their own personal experiences for informational purposes, and it is their Fifth Amendment right to do so. There is no intent to sway the interest of any perspective future employees, or to influence their personal judgment in any one way or another.

Participant number one

I received a call one fateful day, with information about employment testing at a local school campus. The test was for employment with a government agency. I was told to arrive at the testing location at least two hours before the scheduled testing time, because there would be a lot of people there. This call came from my aunt, who seemed to always have an inside scoop on jobs and other helpful information. As instructed, I arrived at the testing location two hours early. Everything was just the way it had been described to me. Even showing up early, there must have been at least a half million people in the line before me for testing.

As I walked up the hill and took my place in line, I looked back to see crowds of more people rushing to join the line. By the scheduled testing time of eight A.M., there must have been at least a million people behind me. I remember thinking inside to myself, "Thank you auntie for advising me well!" I felt blessed to have the position in line that I had. When I finally reached the front of this line, the number assigned to me was under six hundred. I was finished testing and out of there by three P.M. I later learned that the administration continued that day until past nine P.M., and was continued the following day to test all of the attending applicants. During the testing process, there were several forms and applications to complete. The most important

forms, in my opinion, included the questions of which locations and time based appointments

desired. It is important to mark any and all of the offices at which you believe would be best

located for your commute to work daily. It is equally important to mark any and all of the part

time and intermittent employment assignments, this will get you in the door.

Once you have secured a permanent non-probationary position, you may then begin to apply for

full time, post-and-bid, or lateral transfer appointments.

The process from this point was to wait for the test results to be determined. A passing score

would be at seventy percent or higher. There were three parts including office procedure,

remembering what you have read, and basic math. The priority would go to the highest score, so

you would be called in the order from ninety percentile down to the seventy percentile

candidates. The forms completed at testing had lists of government office locations, we marked

all of the locations that we wanted to be assigned to. As each position became vacant, an

application is sent directly to you from the specific hiring office. This application would

probably scare most people by being about fifteen pages long. The previous employment history

alone was at least eight pages long, asking for at least a ten year history. I would fill out the

application, and return it immediately, remembering the huge amount of people who tested for

this position. I knew that the competition was real, and I was determined to beat the rush. I will

never forget the reality while being interviewed, the stack of applications was right there on the

desk. I remember thanking my aunt again inside, for advising me to keep my job because the

process will take a

while to get in. Eventually, I was offered a position in one of my local offices. There was a time lapse of at least one year from the day of testing.

Thinking back on my first day working for the agency, I remember being so excited. I felt glad to be there, and I was eager to learn the ropes. I remember having an underlined fear of making mistakes. There were lots of stories going around about government employees that I had heard over the years, and none of them were very good stories. Most of the stories were about the employees having bad attitudes, and about their lack of commitment. However, I had also heard stories about people who knew someone working for this agency, and how these employees would do things for them. Some said they never stand in line, some said they could pay to get clearance without any documentation, or pass their written tests, and others had said that they could get help clearing fees, or other paperwork issues. Due to my memory of all of the stories that I had heard before being employed here, I kept my guards up. I was very nervous, and I asked a lot of questions until I felt comfortable with agency policy and procedure.

Agency field offices hold weekly meetings between eight a.m. and nine A.M. During my first weekly meeting, I was asked to introduce myself to the crew. I remember stating that I had an extensive background in customer service, and that customer service was my main priority. There were snares and comments from all around me. The statement that I heard then and I remember most now was, "Yeah, we will see how long she keeps that attitude. She will not last around here very long; They are going to wipe that smile right off of her face." There was a group of women who all lived very close to the office, and they were all friends outside of work. It was this group that made those negative statements.

Before long, I began to feel what was described by the group of women in the previously mentioned statements. I soon noticed that I was under surveillance, not only by this group of women, but by the office management as well. I figured that maybe management was just staying close in case I needed support, or to protect me from any lingering negative influences. At first, I didn't take any of it personally, I assumed that these people wanted to help me to grow and learn to do my new job. Eventually, one of the women in the group told me about the position that I had filled. She told me that there was a person caught processing fraudulent applications out of this office. This was the moment I realized that management had been shadowing me, and that maybe I had been under surveillance all this time. It was not just my imagination, and my mind had not been simply playing tricks on me.

As time went by, I became much more familiar with policy and procedure and asked less questions. I was beginning to receive several customer compliments, some of which were sent directly up to headquarters. I was recognized with a certificate of commitment and I was also given a separate sticker for each compliment I received. Over time the sticker numbers got higher, and my confidence grew stronger. I sincerely tried to gain the respect and trust of my peers and the management as well. I did form some good relationships with most of the employees and most of the management team with few exceptions. I was advised by my peers on some things to watch out for, and advised by most of the management team as well.

Suddenly, and all at once, these managers with which whom I had formed good relationships had all left the office. They each left me with words of wisdom, and wished me luck. I later found that one of them had even taken a demotion down to a non-supervisory position because there was no management position available at the exact moment of departure. What this meant in my opinion, was that there was an urgent need to remove their self from something that was present here in this office. I believe it must have been something unspeakable, due to the silent nature of their departure. I also believe that they each wanted me to succeed and that they each stayed just long enough to see me past my probation. It is my belief now that they strategized and protected me from this unspeakable force that was actively present in this office that I had been assigned to.

I would obviously have saved myself the trouble and accepted another assignment had I have known about the unspeakable, right? Do you think that I could have gone to work at a different office and never had been subject to any of this unspeakable in the first place? Answer YES/NO? We can revisit this question later in the story. In addition to the managers who had so suddenly left, I witnessed as at least three employees whom I also had formed good relationships with, resigned their positions outright. My theory is supported by the fact that each of those positions was filled with a person who was strategically used as an instrument against me.

I was scheduled for a training class, and started training at a local office. I was within my second week of a four week training course when the drama first started. I was pulled out of this local training office, and asked to travel more than thirty miles away to join a class already in session. The request confused me, and my training officer too for that matter. Neither of us could understand why I was being snatched out of this convenient location, to be sent so far away. Not to mention the fact that I had already missed half of that class by being sent to the first training. Every teacher runs their own class different from how another teacher would. When I arrived at the new class, I did not receive a warm welcome. I felt that my progress was behind here in this class, as opposed to being told that I was doing extremely well in the first class I had already started elsewhere. I was not really made to feel that I was ever a part of the group, by the trainer or by my class mates.

When it was time to close out our drawers and turn in the money, is when the real drama began. I was not told about the specific way in which this particular office takes the turn-in. By the time my money was finally accepted for turn-in, I had been sent back to redo it about five different times. The control room finally called my trainer to come and show me how to complete their specific turn-in process. All of my class mates had each already been through this process for more than a week by now and were not having any of these procedural issues anymore. I was not present in this training group to experience these issues together as a group, and I did not witness them each while having any issues with learning this new process. While I was being trained on the turn-in procedure, I felt overwhelmed by the lack of patience everyone in this office was showing. They were all very abrasive and short tempered with me. I began to cry, and my training officer made a statement that I will never forget. "I am sorry that you have personal problems at home, but since you are here, you are expected to comply with our rules and regulations." This person also made a specific reference as to which personal problems I was having at home.

This information regarding my family was only shared with one person in confidence, I had told only the manager from my home office whom had arrived to pull me from the previous office during my scheduled training course. I had asked them to please reconsider displacing me, due to a serious illness within my immediate family. That was confidential information, and not anyone besides myself, should have been sharing this private and confidential information with anyone. The next day, the manager from my home office appeared at the training location. I was called out of the training classroom, and led into a room where the training program manager was waiting for me. I was told at that time that I was dismissed from this training class, and that I was instructed to return to my home office immediately.

There was an incident report created in association with these events, and the wording in this report said that my behavior was unacceptable and would not be tolerated. I was still within the imposed one year probationary period at this time, and I was extremely afraid that I would lose my job at that point. It is my opinion now that my written response to that incident report is what saved me. All I did was tell the truth, the truth about me being removed abruptly from a halfway finished course without just cause or explanation, only for me to be thrown into another course more than thirty miles away from home and more importantly, away from my seriously ill immediate relative. I told the truth of the praise that I had received from the first trainer, and the truth of the unwelcome way by which I had been received in the second training. I also wrote the truth about my confidential family information that had been violated by management, and of the malicious way in which it was used against me. And to tell you the truth, I have been writing everything down ever since that day.

There were several events and incident reports that followed the training event, and I rebutted everything that was sent my way with absolution. There were many instances at which this same manager was manipulating my movement within the department. Being hired permanent intermittent, meant that I was required to work the Saturday work shifts. There is a form circulated that we sign to select our preferred Saturday work locations. Naturally, I selected the office closest to my home for me to work at on a Saturday. The truth is that despite which offices I had marked for Saturday service, I was only ever assigned to one specific office every Saturday that I had worked. Despite the fact that I always marked the office located much closer to my home on the form, it was somehow important to the assigning manager for me to be placed in this one specific office. I would get to my home office on the following Monday, and there would be an incident report waiting for me referring to my Saturday service in one negative nature or another.

I later found that this manager had personal relationships with both of these offices and the management in place there, because they had worked in both offices in the past. It was then that I realized how I had been strategically placed in each of these situations intentionally. I felt like I was part of a conspiracy that was deeper than anything I could have ever imagined. Essentially, I was acting out a script that was written for me to play. I was on the famous black list that I had heard coworkers speaking of so many times before. I was learning first hand exactly what being put onto that black list meant. I put in an application for transfer to an office in the area closer to my home, and I was given an interview date and time. However the manager called back and said to me, "I have spoken with your manager, and your interview is cancelled at this time." In my opinion, these managers were all working together, and the unspoken word amongst them is to return the favor whenever it may be needed. I'm basically stuck in a scene straight from the godfather movie.

I began to feel like a different person from who I was before I came to work for the agency. I was constantly watching everything going on around me, and this put extra strain on my everyday personal life. I began to withdraw myself from family and friends and I lacked the energy to do things that I used to enjoy. I had started to feel unhealthy physically, and grey hairs began sprouting from my scalp profusely. My hair had stopped growing, and in fact, I had a small bald area in my head that was growing wider. I began to wear wigs to cover the condition of my hair. Terrible acne formed all over my face, which I thought was peculiar for my age. None of the acne treatment methods were working for me, and I did try them all. I progressively became a heavy cigarette smoker, and none of the methods available to stop smoking worked for me either, not even the medical provider method. I also had by this point gained about one hundred pounds from the time I started working for this agency. My self-esteem was dropping radically, and my personal life was fundamentally suffering.

Before this all started, I had been awarded certificates for perfect attendance, and certificates for receiving no processing discrepancies on any of the work that I had turned in. By the time I wrote this statement your reading now, I had awful attendance. It started with maybe one day absent in the past three months, and it progressed into a week or more absent at a time each month. The vacation and sick time I had built up on the books had all been depleted. I had been to the doctor with symptoms ranging from migraines, to several other physical aches and pains, I often even suffered extreme diarrhea and abdominal discomfort. I was determined there was something dreadfully wrong with me, and felt that I was going to die from it soon without receiving any treatment. The physical tests the doctors performed all showed no results of any illness. I was put on attendance probation status at work, and an attendance memo was placed in my employee file listing all of my many absences.

The most recent pay raise I had received was revoked by management due to poor performance. This raise was already given to me almost six months before it was revoked by management, resulting in an outstanding balance due back to payroll out of my own pocket of more than several hundred dollars. This financial burden was almost immediately following the time when the agency budget fell apart, where we all were furloughed at fourteen percent of our current pay rate. In addition, by the end of the year, a packet was prepared by the office management and sent up to headquarters requesting an adverse action pay reduction be taken against me. This packet included incident reports that clearly stated, "To be removed from employee file after one year." Most of the substantiation included in this action was outdated, and should have been removed from my file long before this action request packet was prepared and submitted. This action, in my opinion, was unmistakably personal. Especially because of the timing, there were three separate actions being taken against me all at once. The intent to negatively affect my welfare was evident to me, at this point. I contacted the union at this point to weigh my options. We fought the action against my pay, and we eventually won! The action was overturned, and ordered to be removed from my record. This entire litigation process had taken up more than one year from start to finish.

The next time I spoke with my doctor, he asked me if I had been under any extra stress lately. I finally spoke to him about the hostile environment and uncomfortable conditions I had been subjected to at work. That is when the doctor found out that I worked for the agency. He immediately referred back into my medical history, with all of the diarrhea and headaches. My doctor immediately referred me to a psychiatrist, stating that I was suffering from stress. The therapy I received informed me that the excessive diarrhea was called irritable bowel syndrome, and that each and every one of the symptoms from which I had been suffering was due to the excessive stress inflicted on me while at work. I was removed from work and placed immediately into therapy at that time. I was relieved to learn that I was not alone in my troubles. I learned that there were several reports of the same behavior at agency offices. This is when I stopped taking it so personally, and I could just focus on my recovery. I am still being treated regularly, and I am taking both depression and anxiety medication daily. My hair still has not grown back, and I am still gaining more weight. I still sometimes ask myself, why did this have to happen to me?

I was finally allowed to transfer from this office into an office that was actually closer to my home. I was enthusiastic about having a fresh start, and I put my best foot forward. My self-esteem began to improve with each passing day. I was almost convinced that the unspeakable had been left behind, and that I was really going to be alright after all. Before long something happened to change my feelings about this transfer, and this fresh start I had hoped to have here in the new office. A bulletin was circulated posting an open management position in the office. I was eligible to apply for this management position, and I was encouraged by some of the office management team to put in an application for the position. I stated to them that I did not think that I was quite ready to step into management at this time. They still were extremely persistent about me submitting the application for a management position in this office. It was at about the same time that I began to notice trouble.

First there were discrepancies with my paperwork, next it was cashiering errors. Then they began to say that my money was short in progressive amounts starting from two dollars and up to over one hundred dollars. Anything valued over fifty dollars is classified as a critical discrepancy, which generates an incident report. I also now noticed that the incident reports were headed with three year retention, rather than the one year retention that was on the heading in the incident reports from my previous unspeakable experiences at the previous office. I can only imagine this change was made due to my overturned action, and the grounds by which I argued and won that case. There were two arguments. How can you use something against me and affect my pay rate today, all of your documentation is out of date? And why don't you have any of my rebuttals which were attached to each incident report that was submitted by management as documentation to warrant this adverse action against me? Remember, I write everything down. And I rebut everything that is sent my way. So I had every one of my written responses available to give the litigation officers for their review and consideration on the case.

There were several requests made by both myself and my doctor, requesting reasonable accommodations and restrictions. None of our requests were honored, and I did not receive any support from the management. I was not even given the ergonomic chair and other work equipment that was needed for me to work comfortably, in addition I was told that I would not be allowed to bring in a chair or equipment that was not purchased through the agency. Gradually, I began on the same downward spiral. The unspeakable is here too, so I had not left anything behind. This was not the fresh start that I had hoped it would be, because there was management present in this office that was connected to my previous office. One of the managers here had worked with managers in the previous office before, in fact, in the Saturday office that I was assigned to. Do you see the connection? Answer YES/NO? These are the type of events that you will encounter here in this agency. I hope that if you choose to come to this side of the fence, you are armed with your repellant and you must keep it with you at all times. Because as soon as you come in unprotected, they smell your fresh blood and they will drain you dry. I no longer have the same enthusiasm for this job that I once had. I feel that this is a good job that carries good medical and dental benefits. I have heard stories from my mother about her job with government, and I also have testimonials from other trusted sources. My aunt worked at one agency for twenty two years only to be laid off only two years short of retirement. She later found that the agency hired three new people with her salary. Even if I leave here to go to the agency that my mom worked for more than 30 years, for more pay to start, they do not offer the full dental and vision that is extended to us here with this agency. And to tell the absolute truth, I have heard even more dreadful stories about them over there.

I have decided for myself, and again, this is simply my personal opinion on my experiences, that I will not let this job worry me. If I start to feel like I am tired, anxious or uncomfortable, then I tell my doctor how I am feeling and he will simply remove me from work until I am stable again. The truth has set me free. I no longer worry as much as I used to about what management may think of me or my performance at work. I don't worry anymore about my attendance, if you are sick then you are just sick. There is nothing that you could do to change the fact that you are not well and simply cannot work in this condition.

When I tell the truth about all of these events I feel a sense of freedom. With each word that I speak, I begin to feel stronger than before. I am not spreading gossip, and I don't believe that you should participate in that type of behavior. However, this information written in this statement are my own personal experiences, and my opinions associated with these experiences. I am sharing this information now because I sincerely believe that it will help future prospective agency employees as well as employees of other large branches of government where these type of issued can arise. Wherever you may go in your quest for success, you may find yourself in a lonely place. If you are alone in a place such as the agency, just remember to always be true to yourself. No matter what comes, you have what it takes inside you to get through. Do not think that you have to go along with the flow, just to get along and survive.

There is no reason to agree with anything that does not feel right to you inside. If it feels wrong, most likely it is, and I have found that there is usually a devil's advocate there to try and convince you to do it. This person will be the one to report the action to authorities just as easily as they talked you into doing the act. Do not trust anyone when it comes to doing favors, or ignoring agency policy.

I also must speak a bit on the people that have learned to live with the dictatorship. This will be the people around you that do not ever seem to be happy unless they are involved in some type of unspeakable behavior. You cannot expect these people to want to hear you speak of your wedding or anniversary plans. Be very careful about sharing too much positive information about yourself or your family, this could get you blacklisted. If you have a nice home and they are still renting, that alone could get you blacklisted. If you have a husband that loves you, and they are all surfing dating sites for blind dates, you know that you are in trouble

Do not speak of your education because most of them only have a GED, a high school diploma is not required to qualify for this position. It is only necessary that you are over eighteen years of age and that you pass the written test and background check. And please for the love of GOD, do not tell them if you have started a small business. The agency pays once per month. Most of us are living paycheck-to-paycheck and are broke by the fifteenth of the month. Now you are an enemy because you will not have to be here forever, you have a way out.

I remember before I got the phone call from my aunt that fateful day. I went into the usual office close to my home where I had always done any of my personal agency business. I found a down to earth, normal everyday type person, and I asked her how to get in.

Her response was hilarious to me at the time, so I could not forget. She replied, "First, you have got to be half crazy, then you go to this website to see when the next testing is." She handed me a paper with the website and phone number on it. Now that all is said and done, that response is not so hilarious after all. I recognize now that she had given me some of the best advice I have ever been given. I now have two reasons why I will never forget that ladies response to such a usual question. People often ask me now, how I got this job. They ask me for information that will help them to get in too. I have always told them everything they need to know, and given them the website and phone numbers to call. I would not be here either, had someone not helped me. "Thanks aunty!"

But now when someone asks I always add, "I will tell you just like that lady told me when I asked her the same question. First you have to be half crazy, because if you are not half crazy already, this job will make you crazy." You will not know how to deal with things that will happen. You would not even know to suspect people of half of the things that they will do. Normal people don't think the worst of everyone, and they usually believe everything people may say unless there is some reason not to. And when there is a transaction that you processed according to the agency records, but you have no recollection of the customer or the situation is not making any sense to you, it is probably because someone has you in their snare and you are about to find out just how far that person will go to see you suffer. This is how I was attacked on several occasions, I learned the hard way of the power given to people with control clearance. The paper work could still have your technician identification number, even when they had made changes from their computer and printed from their own printer. I would never have even known to suspect that this could happen. I will take this opportunity to thank the employee with control clearance that showed me this processing glitch. Thanks for keeping it real with me.

Another clerical lesson came for me on the day that I found out the hard way that management had the power to place another technician into the system with my technician number and their own password. I noticed a jump in my transaction sequence numbers one day while working, I inquired with management as to how this strange occurrence happened. This is when it was revealed that there was two of me both working and collecting money at the same time, but with two different passwords. Of course, they did not tell me much information except that the other technician has been assigned a new number, and that all of the money collected under my code will be turned over to me for my turn in. Watch for borrowed technicians from other offices, or new hires. This could present management with the opportunity to make two of you without you even noticing. They will not tell you if there was a mistake on their part, you have to catch it as it happens. Most of us are simply asked to sign for a cashiering discrepancy and we never ask any questions. This is the reason that I am sharing my experiences, to help you to avoid some of these misfortunes.

Be careful when making friends, the person that you are friends with could be in a snare and you will catch stray bullets by standing too close to them. Also beware of the click, there is always a group that has been there the longest, and live near the office. They will always win the prize in a raffle, or land that job promotion that you were hoping for.

My advice to them now is to expect anything to happen. Believe it when you see it, because it is probably true. Yes, she did do that or yes, he did. Yes, they did it on purpose; it was not an accident. Everything with them is either an accident, or some coincidence. They will even apologize, and it will probably even seem sincere to you at the time.

Don't make yourself sick trying to figure out why they did it. Just make sure you keep your nose clean, and when they come after you, because someone will come after you. Don't be afraid to tell the truth, the truth will set you free, just as it did for me. No matter whom you are or how big you get, there is always someone greater than you think that you are. In other words, giants can fall too. They may scare you at first but if you look within yourself, and you know that you did nothing wrong then you fight back. I do not mean for you to get into a physical altercation while at work, I mean for you to fight with your pen, just like they do.

Anything that is generated by management is placed into your employee file, I am saying that we all have files. If you file a grievance against management for unethical behaviors, that will go into their employee file. If a manager receives enough complaints, it will trigger an investigation into all of their actions. This investigation is what brings giants down, when it is shown that this behavior has repeated itself and has been doing so without notice. There will be consequences to the actions that have been taken outside of agency policy.

There is always someone higher up the ladder than the person who is coming after you. Write everything down, no matter how simple the incident may seem at the time. It could come up again later, and it is never remembered by the other party the same way that you remember it. In fact, it will probably be missing all pieces of information leading to the other party's guilt all together. Do not ever hesitate to speak up for yourself when challenged, and if this fails then use your union, you pay union dues automatically each month out of your payroll as a deduction. Get to know your union book, and keep at least three different union representatives in your speed dial. You will more than likely end up using them all eventually because they are kept busy with employee grievances.

I sincerely wish you the best of luck.